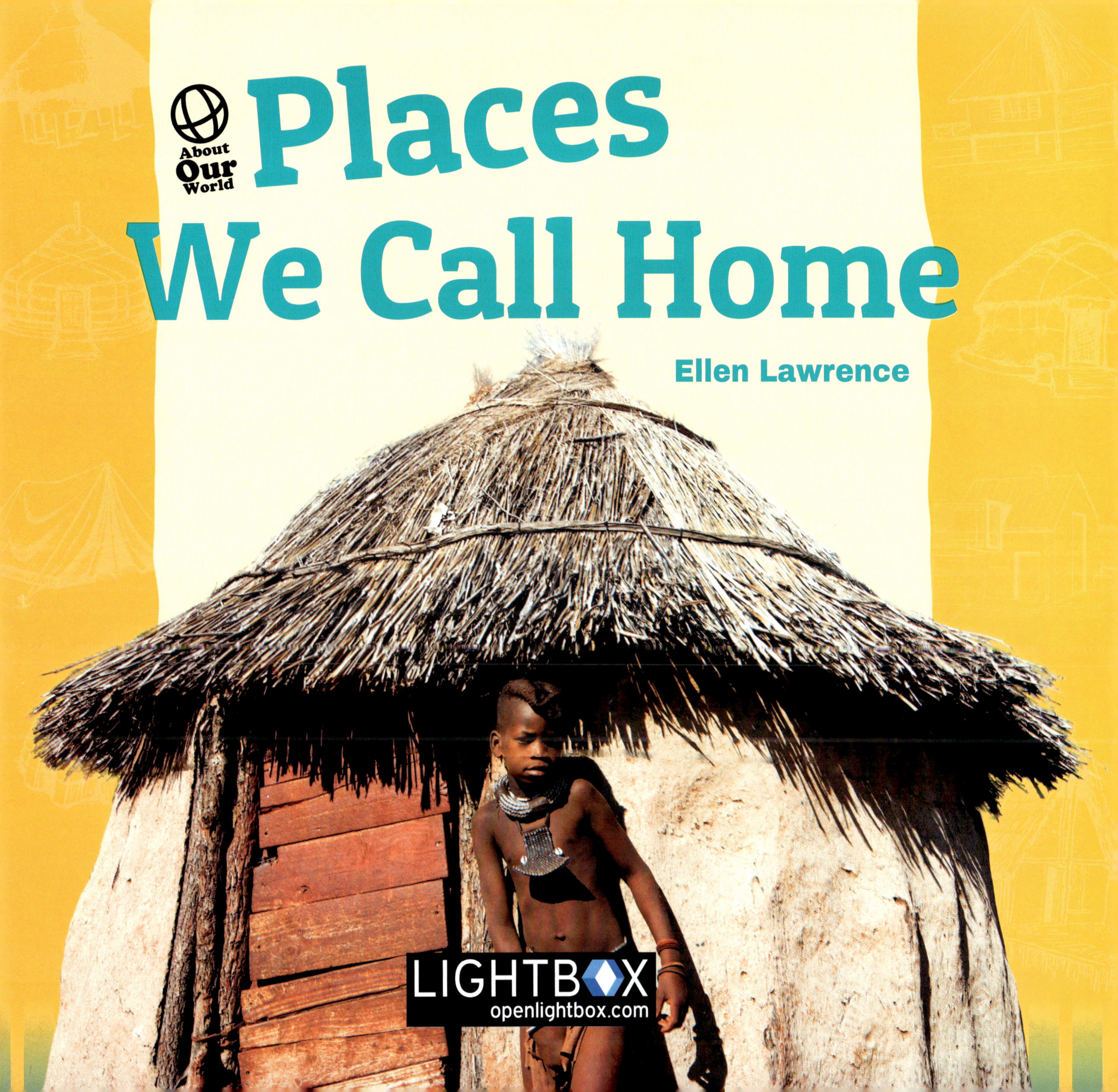
About
Our
World
Places
We Call Home
Ellen Lawrence
LIGHTBOX
openlightbox.com

Go to
www.openlightbox.com
and enter this book's
unique code.

ACCESS CODE

LBA93554

Lightbox is an all-inclusive digital solution for the teaching and learning of curriculum topics in an original, groundbreaking way. Lightbox is based on National Curriculum Standards.

OPTIMIZED FOR

- ✓ **TABLETS**
- ✓ **WHITEBOARDS**
- ✓ **COMPUTERS**
- ✓ **AND MUCH MORE!**

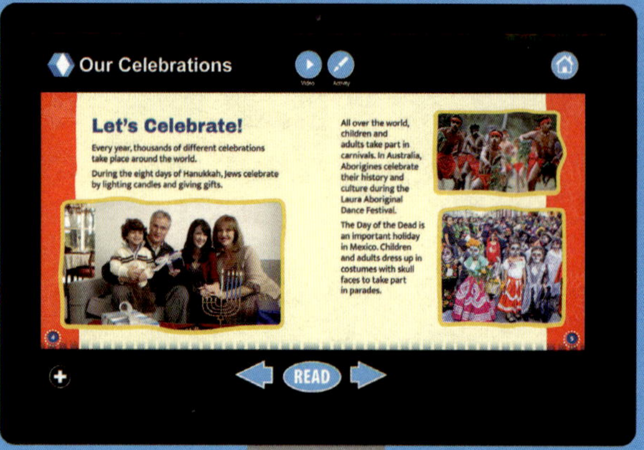

STANDARD FEATURES OF LIGHTBOX

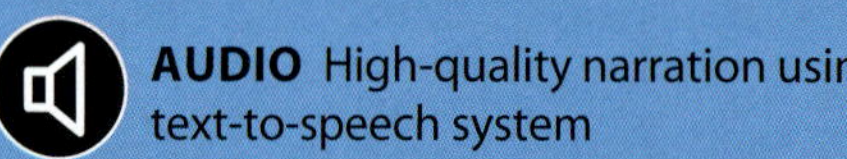
AUDIO High-quality narration using text-to-speech system

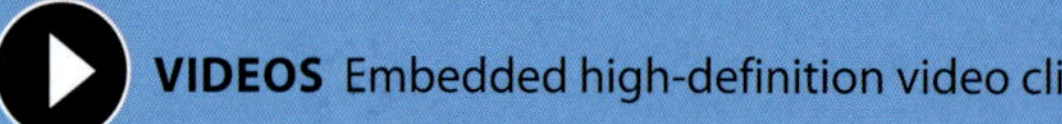
VIDEOS Embedded high-definition video clips

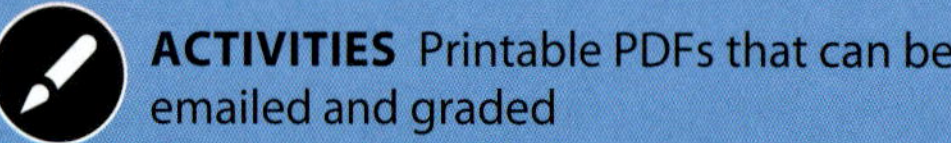
ACTIVITIES Printable PDFs that can be emailed and graded

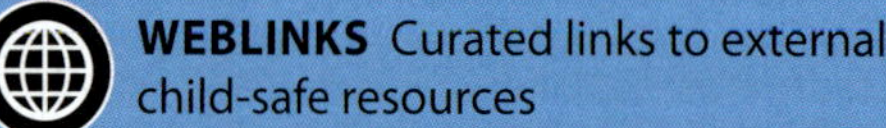
WEBLINKS Curated links to external, child-safe resources

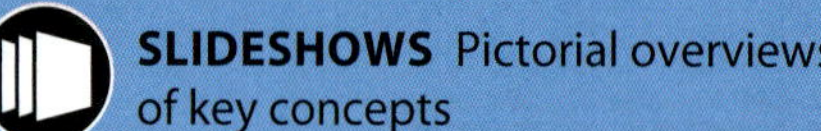
SLIDESHOWS Pictorial overviews of key concepts

INTERACTIVE MAPS Interactive maps and aerial satellite imagery

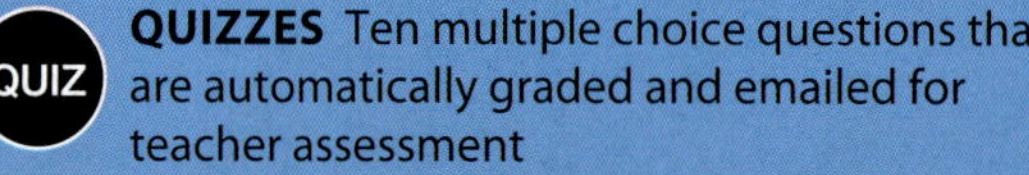
QUIZZES Ten multiple choice questions that are automatically graded and emailed for teacher assessment

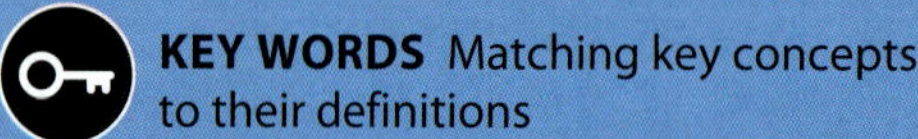
KEY WORDS Matching key concepts to their definitions

VIDEOS

WEBLINKS

SLIDESHOWS

QUIZZES

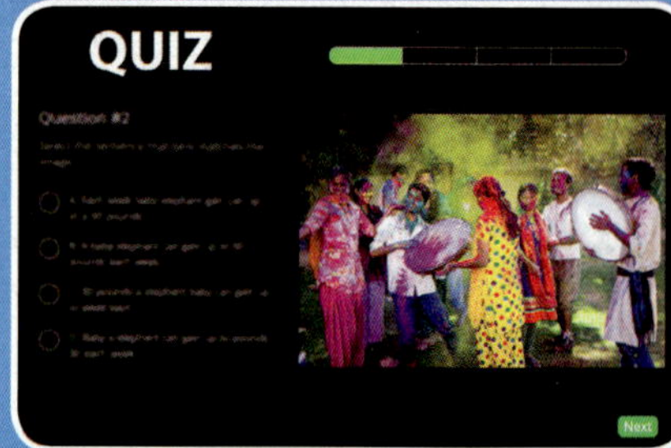

About Our World

Places We Call Home

What Is a Home?

A home is a place to stay cool. A home is a place to stay warm. A home is a place to stay dry.

A home is a place to be with the people you love. A home is a place to feel safe.

Everybody needs a place to call home.

A Himba Hut

The Himba people of Namibia live in small villages. Sometimes they move from place to place to find grass for their goats and cattle.

Wherever they settle, Himba people build small homes called huts. The huts are made of branches covered with dried mud and cow dung.

When Himba children are very young, they live and sleep in a hut with their parents. Once they are about three years old, they leave their parents' hut. Then they share a hut with other children.

Many Himba people live in the Namib desert. This desert runs 1,200 miles (1,900 kilometers) along the coast of Africa.

A Floating Village

On a huge lake in Cambodia, people live in floating villages. The lake is called Tonlé Sap (TUHN-lay SAHP). The children who live here travel to their schools by boat. At lunchtime, they buy food from a floating food cart.

Some families make their homes in houses that float on the water. Others live on houseboats. Some of the homes on the lake have floating gardens. There are floating shops, gas stations, churches, and even floating basketball courts!

Rainbow Homes in the Snow

On the tiny island of Kulusuk, the land turns white in winter. There's still a rainbow of colors to be seen, however.

That's because everyone on Kulusuk lives in brightly painted wooden houses.

Kulusuk is just off the coast of Greenland. The island is home to fewer than 300 people.

Almost no trees grow in Greenland, so there's no wood for construction. All the pieces of a house are sent by boat from Denmark. Then the owners fit the pieces together to make their new home.

Lots of sled dogs live on Kulusuk. They pull the sleds that people use to travel over the ice and snow.

Living in a City

Around the world, billions of people live in big cities. A city can be a noisy place with lots of traffic jams.

Some people in a city live in houses. Many city homes do not have a garden or yard. People spend time outdoors in parks and playgrounds.

Many people in cities live in apartments high above the ground.

The city of Buenos Aires, Argentina, has more than 250 parks and green spaces.

A Home in a City Slum

Not everybody who lives in a city has a house or apartment. Around the world, millions of very poor people make their homes in parts of cities known as slums.

In the city of Delhi in India, thousands of people live in slums. They build small homes from materials they find on the streets and in garbage dumps.

The homes have no electricity, toilets, or water for drinking, cooking, and washing.

In Delhi, thousands of families may share just one water tap in a slum area. Each day, adults and children stand in line for hours to fill buckets and plastic bottles with water from the tap.

A House with a Tower

On the Indonesian island of Sumba, people live in small villages. Each village is made up of houses that have towers on the roofs.

The people of Sumba are farmers. They raise pigs, water buffaloes, and chickens. Animals live in the bottom part of the house.

The tower of a Sumba house is used as a safe place to keep precious objects. People believe that the spirits of their ancestors live in the towers of their homes.

The roof of a Sumba house is made of grass or leaves. It has to be redone every five years.

A Home on the Move

Many people in Mongolia raise horses, cattle, camels, sheep, and goats. They are nomads who move from place to place to find fresh grass for their animals.

When you're on the move, you need a home that can move, too. Mongolian nomads live in tent-like homes called *gers*. It takes less than an hour to build or dismantle a ger!

People in Mongolia have lived in gers for at least 3,000 years. A ger has a wooden frame. The frame is covered with layers of felt made from sheep's wool. It has an outer covering made from waterproof canvas.

A Place to Call Home

Every year, many people around the world have to leave their homes. Sometimes this happens because of a natural disaster such as a flood or earthquake. Sometimes it's because of war.

In 2011, a war began in Syria. Millions of people left their homes to escape from danger.

They became refugees and had to find safety in camps in Syria and in neighboring countries.

Many refugees live in a camp for years. They hope that one day it will be safe to go home.

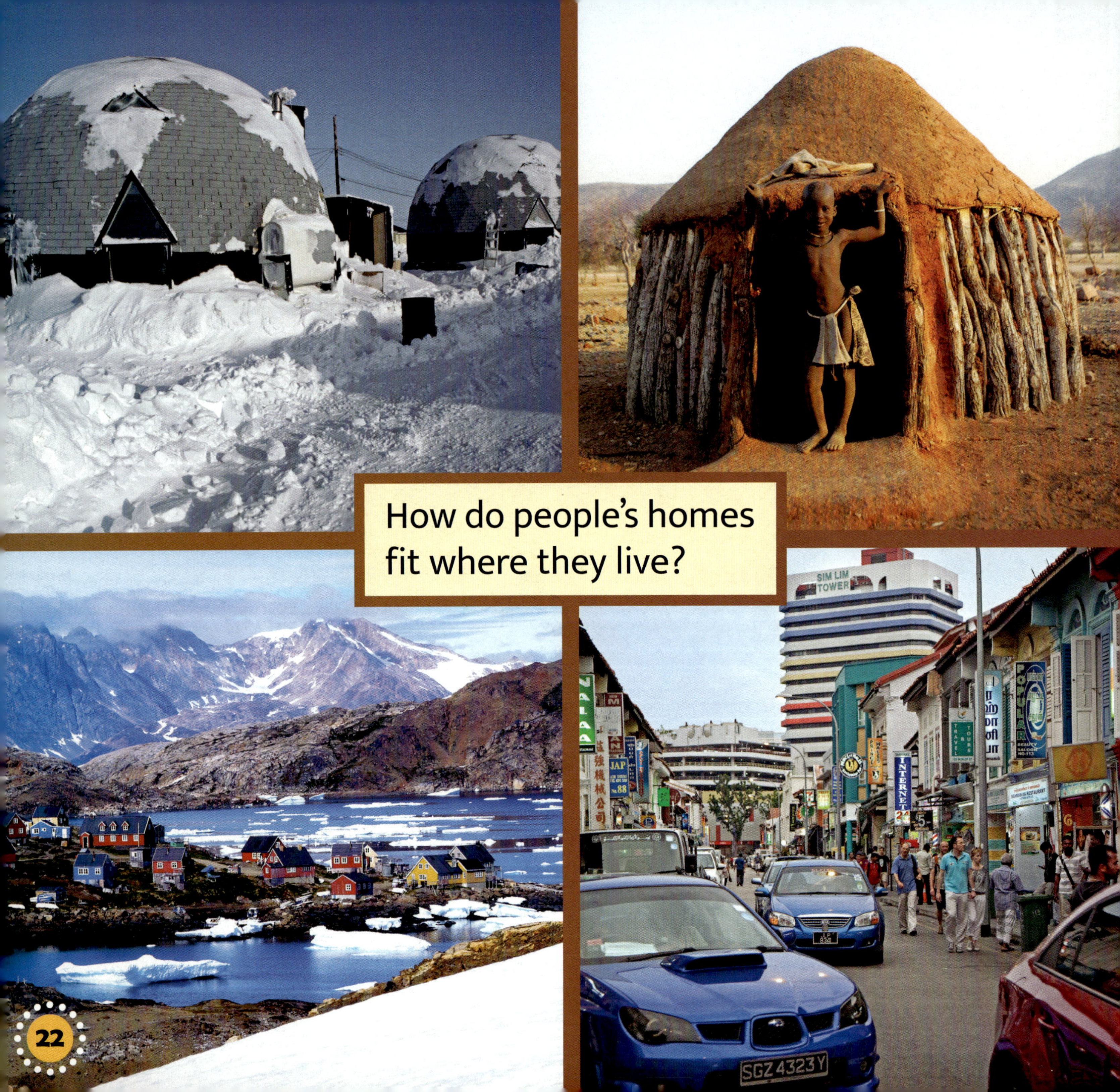

How do people's homes fit where they live?

How are these homes like yours? How are they different?

KEY WORDS

Research has shown that as much as 65 percent of all written material published in English is made up of 300 words. These 300 words cannot be taught using pictures or learned by sounding them out. They must be recognized by sight. This book contains 120 common sight words to help young readers improve their reading fluency and comprehension. This book also teaches young readers several important content words, such as proper nouns. These words are paired with pictures to aid in learning and improve understanding.

Page	Sight Words First Appearance
4	a, home, is, place, to, what
5	be, call, needs, people, the, with, you
6	and, are, find, for, from, in, live, made, move, of, small, sometimes, their, they
7	about, along, children, leave, many, miles, old, once, other, runs, then, this, three, very, when, years, young
8	at, by, food, here, on, schools, who
9	even, have, houses, make, seen, some, that, there, turns, water
10	because, just, land, off, still, than, white
11	all, almost, grow, new, no, over, so, together, trees, use
12	around, big, can, city, world
13	above, do, has, high, more, not, or, time
14	as, known, parts
15	day, each, line, may, one
16	animals, up
17	every, it, keep
18	an, like, takes, too
20	began, had, it's, left, such
21	go, will
22	how, where
23	different, these, yours

Page	Content Words First Appearance
6	branches, cattle, dung, goats, grass, Himba, huts, mud, Namibia, villages
7	Africa, children, coast, desert
8	boat, Cambodia, cart, lake, lunchtime, Tonlé Sap
9	basketball, churches, courts, houseboats, gardens, gas stations
10	island, Kulusuk, Greenland, rainbow, snow, winter
11	construction, Denmark, dogs, ice, sled
12	cities, traffic jams
13	apartments, Argentina, Buenos Aires, parks, playgrounds, yard
14	Delhi, garbage dumps, India, materials, slums, streets
15	adults, bottles, buckets, electricity, hours, tap, toilets, plastic
16	chickens, farmers, Indonesian, pigs, roofs, Sumba, tower, water buffaloes
17	ancestors, leaves, spirits
18	camels, cattle, gers, goats, horses, Mongolia, nomads, sheep
19	canvas, felt, frame, wool
20	camps, countries, danger, earthquake, flood, refugees, safety, Syria

Published by Smartbook Media Inc.
350 5th Avenue, 59th Floor New York, NY 10118
Website: www.openlightbox.com

Printed in the United States of America in Brainerd, Minnesota
1 2 3 4 5 6 7 8 9 0 22 21 20 19 18

012018
120117

Library of Congress Cataloging in Publication Control Number: 2017959803

ISBN 978-1-5105-3542-8 (hardcover)
ISBN 978-1-5105-3543-5 (multi-user eBook)

Project Coordinator: John Willis
Art Director: Terry Paulhus

Every reasonable effort has been made to trace ownership and to obtain permission to reprint copyright material. The publisher would be pleased to have any errors or omissions brought to its attention so that they may be corrected in subsequent printings.
The publisher acknowledges Getty Images and Alamy as its primary image suppliers for this title.